Meet NASA Inventor Anthony Longman and His Team's

Expandable Space Habitat

WORLD BOOK

www.worldbook.com

World Book, Inc.
180 North LaSalle Street
Suite 900
Chicago, Illinois 60601
USA

For information about other World Book publications, visit our website at www.worldbook.com or call 1-800-WORLDBK (967-5325).

For information about sales to schools and libraries, call 1-800-975-3250 (United States), or 1-800-837-5365 (Canada).

Produced in collaboration with the National Aeronautics and Space Administration (NASA).

Library of Congress Cataloging-in-Publication Data for this volume has been applied for.

Out of This World
ISBN: 978-0-7166-6261-7 (set, hc.)

Expandable Space Habitat
ISBN: 978-0-7166-6267-9 (hc.)
ISBN: 978-0-7166-6283-9 (pf.)

Also available as:
ISBN: 978-0-7166-6275-4 (e-book)

Staff

Editorial

Director
Tom Evans

Manager, New Content
Jeff De La Rosa

Writer
William D. Adams

Proofreader/Indexer
Nathalie Strassheim

Graphics and Design

Senior Visual
Communications Designer
Melanie Bender

Media Researcher
Rosalia Bledsoe

Acknowledgments

Cover   © Robert S, Shutterstock; Anthony Longman
4-5   © Marcel Clemens, Shutterstock
6-7   Rick Guidice, NASA
9   NASA
11   © Raymond Cassel, Shutterstock
12-13   Anthony Longman; Architectural Archives, University of Pennsylvania
14-15   Don Davis, NASA
16-17   Buzz Aldrin, NASA; Hawkeye7 (licensed under CC BY-SA 4.0); © Rebecca Hale, National Geographic
18-19   Anthony Longman
21   © Ver0nicka/Shutterstock
22-23   © CasarsaGuru/Getty Images; Ben Stephenson (licensed under CC BY 2.0)

25   Henk Monster (licensed under CC BY 3.0)
27   Sunspiral (licensed under CC BY-SA 4.0)
28-29   Rick Guidice, NASA
31   Anthony Longman
33   © TransAstra
35   Anthony Longman, © Sky vectors/Shutterstock
36-37   Anthony Longman
38-39   Peter Rubin, Iron Rooster Studios/Skyframe Research & Development
41-43   Anthony Longman
44   Library of Congress; Johann Sebastian Bach (1746), oil on canvas by Elias Gottlob Haussmann; Museum of City History Leipzig

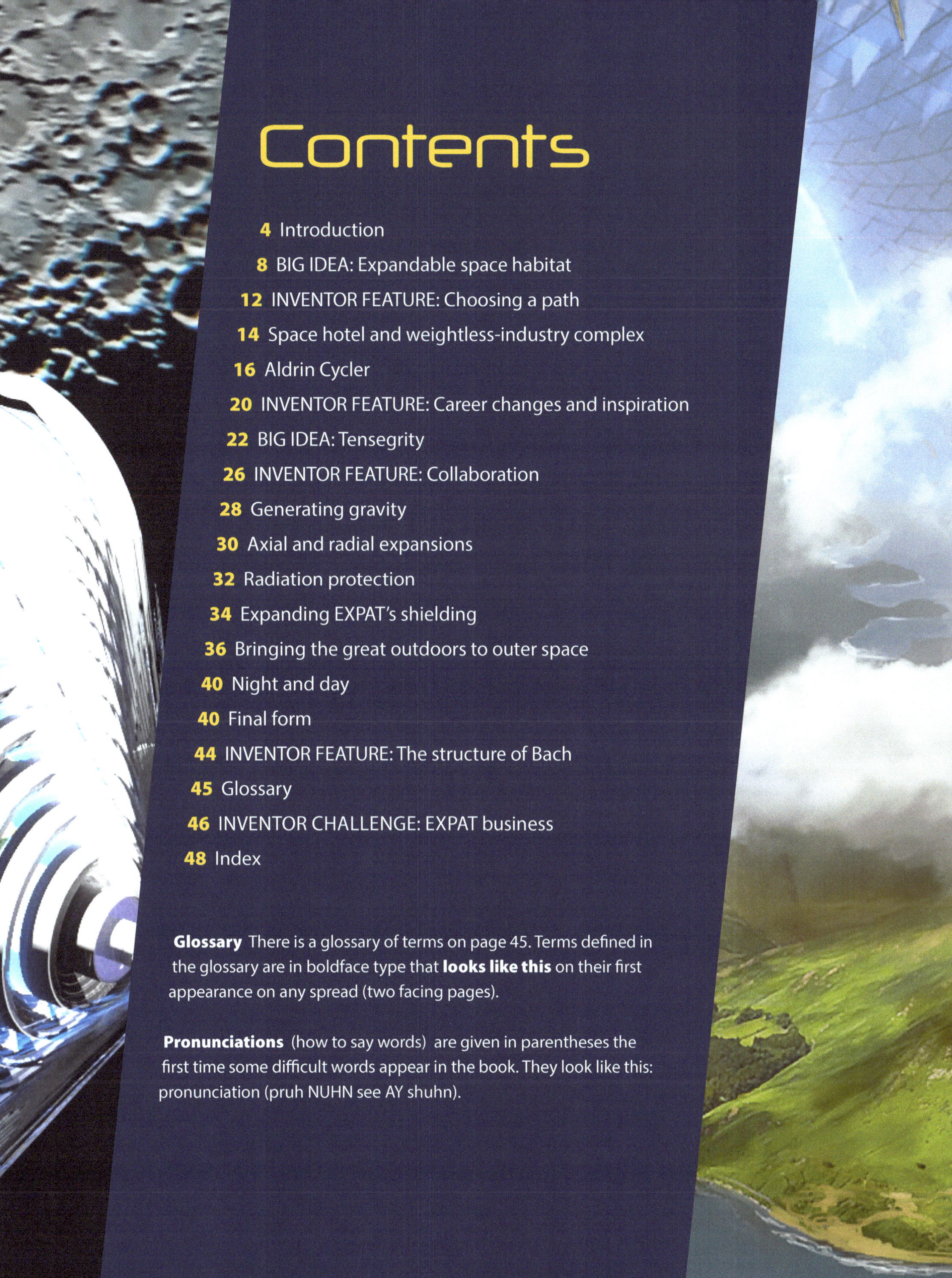

Contents

Glossary There is a glossary of terms on page 45. Terms defined in the glossary are in boldface type that **looks like this** on their first appearance on any spread (two facing pages).

Pronunciations (how to say words) are given in parentheses the first time some difficult words appear in the book. They look like this: pronunciation (pruh NUHN see AY shuhn).

Introduction

The International Space Station (ISS) is a marvel of **engineering.** It provides enough space for six astronauts to live and work in **orbit** around Earth. Protective shielding and life-support systems keep them safe. The ISS is the cushiest home ever built in space, complete with private sleeping quarters, an exercise room, and even a few space-grown vegetables!

Though it may seem like a palace in space, the ISS has about as much room as three average Earth homes. And, its building was a colossal undertaking, involving dozens of rocket launches over more than a decade. At a cost of over $100 billion, it is the single most expensive structure humans have ever created. Multiple rocket launches a year are needed to ferry supplies, experiments, and astronauts to and from the station.

Meanwhile, commercial interest in space is at an all-time high. Swarms of new satellites are coming online. Tourists are willing to pay big money to get a taste of space travel. Inventors are coming up with ways to harvest resources on **asteroids** or to take advantage of weightless conditions to manufacture novel materials in space.

It makes little sense to live in Australia if you have to commute to work in the United States. The cost and time of travel are far too great. Likewise, if we are to take advantage of all the opportunities that space offers, more people will probably have to live and work in space.

The space dwellers of the future will need more than just a few more space stations in low Earth **orbit,** with supplies and personnel shuttled back and forth to the surface. They will require true space habitats, with plenty of room to comfortably live, work, and even grow the food they need far from Earth. In short, they're going to need more space in space.

Engineer Anthony Longman is working to provide that space. The space station Longman envisions would not be constructed piece by piece over multiple rocket launches. Instead, his expanding space habitat could be launched by a single rocket, later to grow and spread with the needs of its inhabitants.

The NASA Innovative Advanced Concepts program. The titles in the *Out of This World* series feature projects that have won grant money from a group formed by the United States National Aeronautics and Space Administration, or NASA. The NASA Innovative Advanced Concepts program (NIAC) provides funding to teams working to develop bold new advances in space technology. You can visit NIAC's website at www.nasa.gov/niac.

NIAC
NASA Innovative Advanced Concepts

Meet Anthony Longman.
I'm an architect and **landscape architect** by training, but I'm also fascinated by space, ecology, and mathematics. Today, I'm designing an expandable habitat for people to live and work—and even raise families—in space!

People have dreamed of living in space for decades, but the high cost of building and maintaining living quarters there has kept it mostly as a dream. Small habitations like the International Space Station (ISS) require billions of dollars of life-support equipment and constant resupply. Larger habitats could cost less per inhabitant and be more self-sufficient. But such a habitat could take dozens of rocket launches and unimaginable sums of money to complete.

" I realized that we had to figure out a way to get there from a growth process. **"** —Anthony

Longman is working to develop a space habitat that can be launched into position by a single heavy-lift rocket, the likes of which will be available in the next couple of years.

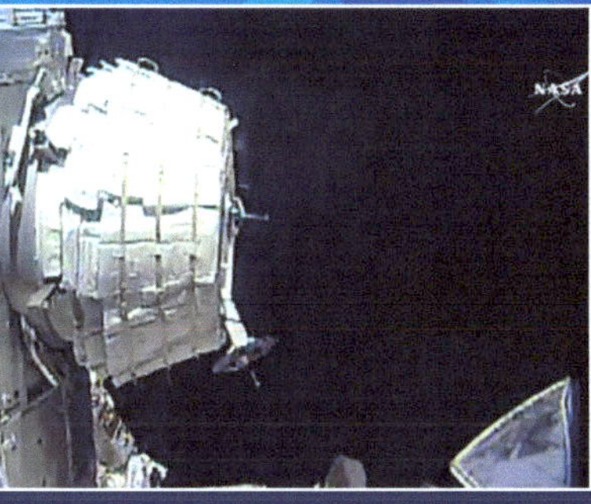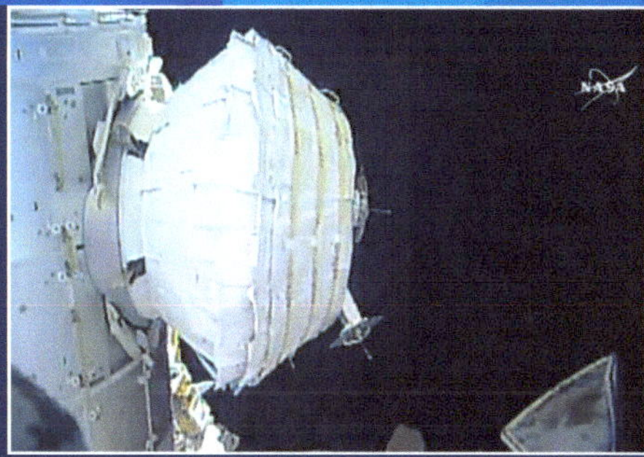

The Bigelow Expandable Activity Module (BEAM) is inflated at the ISS. The BEAM is a prototype designed to test the performance of such air-filled expandable space station modules.

> **The key thing is to realize that you can start really small. The original deployed version of the habitat is small enough that it can be launched on a single rocket.** —Anthony

Longman's habitat will be expandable. He doesn't imagine a maze of modular components launched individually and cobbled together in space. Instead, the first launch will carry nearly everything the station will need to operate and expand. The craft will then grow according to a predetermined plan, designed to minimize disruption to its residents and provide the most value. Longman calls his concept the Expandable Shielded Rotating Space Habitat, or EXPAT for short.

EXPAT could be launched by Blue Origin's New Glenn rocket, SpaceX's Super Heavy rocket, or NASA's Space Launch System, all of which are in active development. A single launch could carry the main structure into space, although a few more might be needed to outfit EXPAT for human habitation—and to deliver its first inhabitants.

Much of the specialized equipment and materials that make up the station would be shipped from Earth. But as EXPAT grows, the station would also harvest materials it needs in large quantities from **asteroids** or the moon. This strategy will be much cheaper than launching bulky materials from Earth. But, the success of EXPAT will depend upon the development of asteroid and lunar mining technologies. In its early stages, EXPAT might house some of the first asteroid miners, serve as a workshop for companies developing products in a weightless environment, or entertain visiting space tourists.

What's in a name?

Expat is short for *expatriate,* a person who lives somewhere other than where they were born—outer space, in this case!

Artist's illustration of a probe harvesting materials from an asteroid

Inventor Feature:
Choosing a path

Longman as a child

Longman grew up in the United Kingdom. As a teenager, he had to choose between studying the sciences and the humanities, due to the structure of the school system.

Longman chose the sciences, but he maintained a strong interest in other subjects.

Soon, Longman discovered architecture and **landscape architecture.** Landscape architecture is a profession that involves the design and development of land for human use and enjoyment. It is concerned with the beauty of natural surroundings as well as practical ways to use land and the objects on it. Longman spent a year at the University of Pennsylvania studying under the Scottish-born landscape architect Ian McHarg. McHarg's 1969 book *Design with Nature* was the first book to combine environmentalism with landscape architecture and urban design.

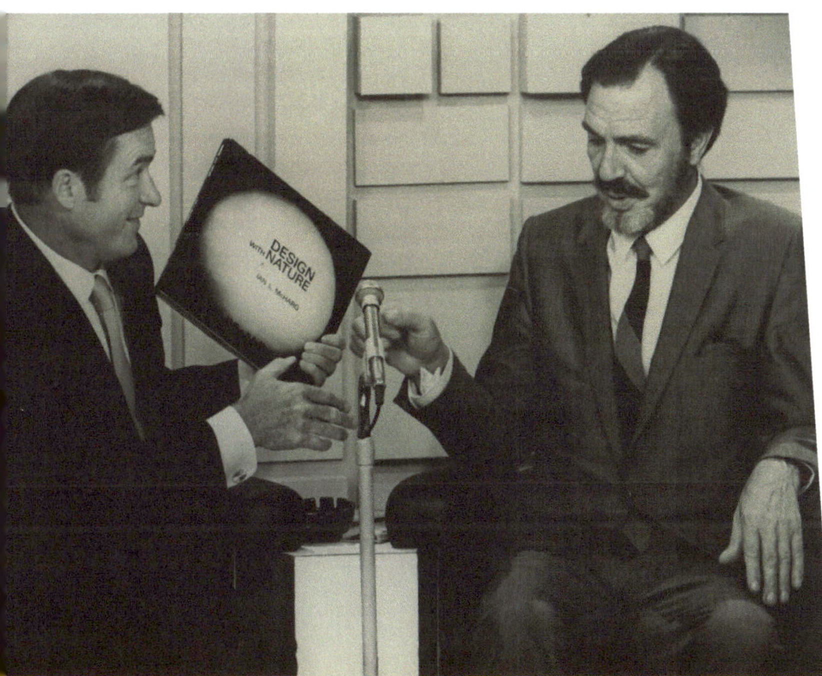

Ian McHarg (right) describes his book *Design with Nature* on a television program.

Space hotel and weightless-industry complex

Many people wish to go to space for the thrill of it. Such companies as Blue Origin and Virgin Galactic are working to offer brief, suborbital spaceflights to paying customers. Many thousands of people have signed up for a waiting list, made a down payment, or even paid in full. There is likely a similar demand for more extended stays in space. In the 2000's, seven people paid tens of millions of dollars each to travel to space and spend several days aboard the International Space Station (ISS).

EXPAT aims to be more than just a space hotel, however. The station could also generate rent from manufacturing and medical companies.

Aboard an **orbiting** station, objects exist in a state of freefall—that is, they are freely falling to the Earth, though their sideways motion prevents them from plummeting to the ground. Freefall conditions give rise to an experience of weightlessness. On such an orbiting station, for example, objects don't fall to the floor when dropped, and lighter gases don't rise.

Weightless conditions enable the manufacture of novel materials that cannot be made under surface conditions on Earth. These may include high-tech fiber-optic cables, special drugs, and even artificial replacement organs. EXPAT could provide a weightless industrial zone for this work, along with a place for the workers to live.

You could sell apartments to the hundred or thousand wealthiest people on Earth and fund an entire space station. —Anthony

Cycler

Another way EXPAT could be profitable is as a **cycler.**

From 1969 to 1972, NASA landed a dozen astronauts on the moon over the course of six missions as part of the Apollo program. It was widely assumed that the program would eventually lead to a permanent human presence on the moon and the first steps towards sending humans to Mars. However, shifting political priorities and slashed budgets kept these plans on the drawing board.

The American astronaut Buzz Aldrin was the second person to set foot on the moon. In 1985, frustrated by a lack of progress in human spaceflight, Aldrin proposed to establish a more permanent connection to the moon or Mars. He envisioned a large spacecraft or space station placed in a carefully planned **orbit** so that it might cycle between Earth and the moon or Earth and Mars without needing much fuel. Such a craft—as well as the orbit it circles in—is called a cycler.

A Mars cycler orbits (shown here green) in such a way that it encounters Mars and Earth twice during each of its orbits (image is not to scale).

A lunar **cycler** would travel in an *elongated* (stretched out) **orbit** around Earth. Think of a cycler as something like a train running on a continuous loop to the moon and back. It would take about a week for the cycler to travel from Earth to the moon and another three weeks for it to return. Passengers and freight could be ferried by a shuttle to the cycler, hitching a ride to the moon. There, another shuttle could lower them to the lunar surface.

A weeklong cruise to the moon may sound fun, but a three-week return cruise could be a drag. To shorten the return time, another cycler could be launched to orbit in the opposite direction, taking a week to get from the moon to Earth and three weeks to get back. With enough demand, more cyclers could be added in each direction, providing for regular, reliable lunar excursions.

Providing trips to the moon could be a great source of income for the newly launched EXPAT. A cycler orbit from Earth to Mars is even more intriguing. Such an orbit might pass close to **asteroids** near the main asteroid belt, providing access to valuable resources. A fully expanded EXPAT would have a capacity of about 8,000 people, almost as much as the largest cruise ships.

In this illustration, a fully expanded EXPAT is being used as a lunar cycler.

" This could be a cruise ship. It could be an ocean liner between Earth and Mars. " —Anthony

Longman moved to California in 1981 and worked as an architect. In the late 1980's, he bought a computer and began to learn computer-aided design (CAD), which was becoming an important tool for architecture. Through a contact in Hollywood, he began to work in the film industry, using CAD to sketch out three-dimensional roughs of complex scenes. Longman's sketches enabled directors and producers to see what a scene might look like before spending lots of money on complex visual effects. Longman spent much of the 1990's creating graphics for movies, video games, documentaries, and even courtroom animations. At the end of the 1990's, as the field got more crowded, he returned to architecture.

Inspiration struck in 2007, when Longman and his wife moved to a new house in Southern California with a spectacular view.

People have come up with designs for space habitats before. The most influential of these designs is that of the American physicist Gerard K. O'Neill. It featured vast, rotating cylinders with alternating strips of occupied living space and glass windows. EXPAT shares some of these features. But O'Neill's cylinders were not designed to grow with their inhabitants.

How can a space habitat have the ability to grow?

Tensegrity is short for *tensional integrity*. Those are pretty big words, but the concept is relatively simple. A structure that takes advantage of tensegrity is made up of two different elements: rigid *struts* (supports) and flexible cables. The rigid struts do not touch one another. Instead, they are connected by the cables, which hold the structure together through tension. Think of it as something like an arrangement of rigid poles held together by a spiderweb of cables.

Tensegrity structures are extremely strong because the only stresses present are compression in the struts and tension in the cables. Think of a strut like a wooden dowel. It's pretty easy to break a dowel by bending it, perhaps over your knee. It's much more difficult

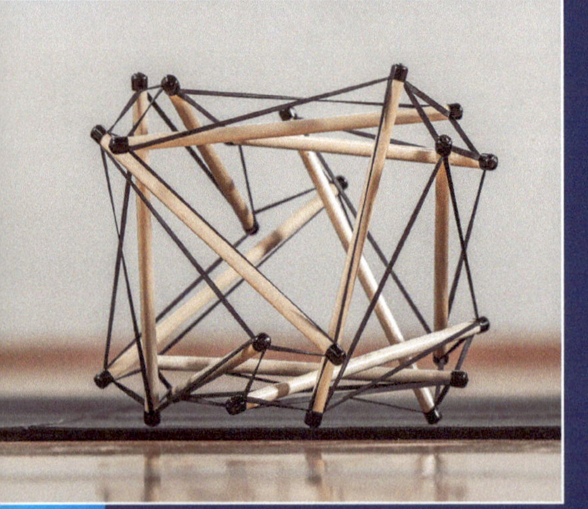

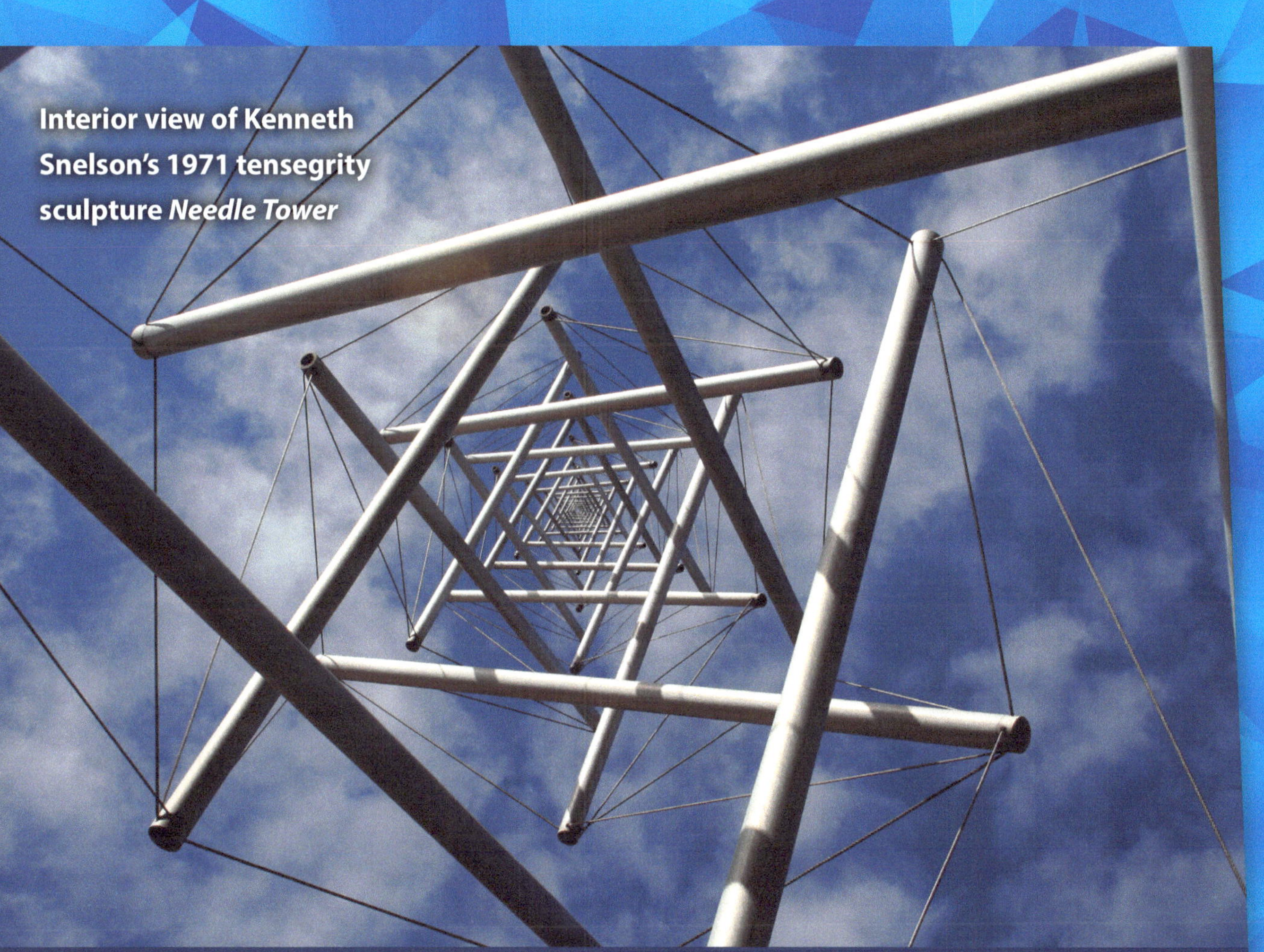

to break it through compression, by pushing the two ends into each other. Likewise, think of the cables like strings. It's pretty easy to break a string by cutting it or applying other pressure from the side. It's much more difficult to break the string using tension, by stretching the two ends apart.

> **What you have is a structure comprised of pure tensions in the cables and pure compression in the struts. There are no bending forces.** —Anthony

Tensegrity was popularized by Buckminster Fuller and Kenneth Snelson in the 1950's and 1960's. Fuller, an American **engineer,** coined the term *tensegrity.* He poetically described the concept as "islands of compression in a sea of tension." Snelson, an American artist, studied under Fuller. He produced a variety of amazing tensegrity sculptures that seem to float in air.

Since Fuller and Snelson, **engineers** have used elements of tensegrity in the design of some buildings. The canopies of many sports stadiums, for example, have been built using elements of tensegrity. This is because tensegrity structures are strong and lightweight, enabling them to cover a large area efficiently.

Tensegrity structures have another interesting property. If one or more of the cables is lengthened or shortened, the structure changes shape until compression and tension reach a new balance point. It is this property that will enable EXPAT to expand after launch.

Down to Earth:

Ideas from space that could serve us on our planet.

Tensegrity has plenty of uses here on Earth. Militaries are investigating using tensegrity to create emergency structures that can be deployed very quickly. Tensegrity-inspired structures could even serve as permanent, high-altitude, airborne platforms for research and communication purposes.

Inventor Feature:
Collaboration

Longman knew he could not fully develop such a huge project as EXPAT by himself. Instead, he turned to collaborations with other people involved in the NIAC program.

Tensegrity structures are extremely complex, seeming to defy traditional laws of physics. At first, Longman struggled to model his station mathematically.

> I just knew that there had to be a way to do it. A big turning point was when I was introduced to Professor Bob Skelton. —Anthony

Skelton, who lived in nearby San Diego, had come up with a mathematics system and computer programs to calculate and model tensegrity structures. Longman went to visit and told Skelton about his idea.

The two struck up a partnership to further develop EXPAT.

Through the NIAC program, Longman was also introduced to Joel Sercel. Sercel is an American *entrepreneur* (business developer) who has secured several NIAC grants for studying mining asteroids and the moon. Longman and Sercel realized their projects would benefit each other and collaborated to improve them.

—Anthony

Tensegrobot?

In another NIAC-funded study, **engineers** led by Adrian Agogino developed a **prototype** robot based on tensegrity. The robot consists of several struts connected with cables. Motors on the ends of the struts can lengthen and shorten the cables, enabling the robot to change shape and roll around. Its flexibility makes it resistant to hard landings. And, it can fold itself into a flat triangle, taking up little space in a launch vehicle.

Generating gravity

The weightless conditions experienced by astronauts may look like fun, but they can get you down after a while. Humans need **gravitation** to grow and function properly. Astronauts who spend months living in space return to Earth with brittle bones, weakened muscles, blurred vision, and other ailments. For the long-term health of space dwellers, a habitat will therefore need to generate artificial gravity.

Artificial gravity may sound complicated, but it's actually fairly easy to pull off—you just need a little spin. Maybe you have twirled a bucket full of water by the handle. If you twirl the bucket fast enough, the water won't fall out, even when the bucket is upside down. It is the water's *inertia* (resistance to changes in its motion) that holds it to the bucket. But from the water's point of view, some unseen "force" seems to be holding it into the bucket. This effect is sometimes called "centrifugal force."

Now imagine a space station like a giant cylinder or tube, spinning around its axis. The station and the astronauts and everything else on board all spin together. Just like the water in the bucket, the astronauts will feel a "force" pulling them to the outer wall of the station. The "centrifugal force" they feel is actually just an effect of their inertia. But it is enough to replace the pull of gravity, holding them to the surface of the tube like a giant, curved floor.

Artist's illustration of an O'Neill cylinder. The cylinder would rotate, generating artificial gravity for the inhabitants. EXPAT will create artificial gravity in the same way.

Axial and radial expansions

To provide artificial **gravity,** the inhabited part of EXPAT
will be rotating about an axis. The station will be able
to expand in two directions: *axial* (along the axis of
rotation) and *radial* (outward from the axis of rotation).

Both directions of expansion are important. First, EXPAT
will undergo a number of axial expansions, growing
longer. Then, it will undergo a long series of alternating
axial and radial expansions.

EXPAT will expand to the point at which it can provide
standard Earth gravity at its outermost inhabited layer
while spinning at a rate of two rotations per minute.
(Rotating any faster than this might replace the comfy
sensation of artificial gravity with the nausea of being
spun on a carnival ride!) At this point, the craft will be
about 734 feet (224 meters) in diameter at the habitable
layer. Once EXPAT reaches this diameter, the station will
expand axially, broadening its habitable surface.

All this expansion must take place while people
continue to live and work aboard EXPAT. This continuous
habitation will enable the station to remain profitable.

Cutaway model of EXPAT.
Sections will be added in a
particular sequence to make
the best use of resources
and to avoid disrupting the
lives of the inhabitants.

Radiation protection

Space is full of harmful **radiation**. Earth's **atmosphere** and **magnetic field** shield us from much of it here on the surface. But there's no such protection far beyond Earth **orbit.** Harmful radiation can easily penetrate the hull of a spaceship, damaging living cells and leading to an increased risk of cancer and early death.

Instead of some high-tech shielding system, Longman proposes to protect the inhabitants of EXPAT with something simple: dirt and water. But these heavy materials will not be launched from Earth. Instead, they will be mined from **asteroids.**

Joel Sercel and others are already working on plans to extract water from asteroids. Such water could be processed into spacecraft **propellant.** But water is also effective at blocking certain kinds of radiation.

Many asteroids are also covered in a thick layer of loose rock, sand, and dust called **regolith.** Regolith cannot be used to build or refuel spaceships, so it should be fairly cheap. A thick layer of regolith in the outer hull could help protect the EXPAT from both radiation and impacts from space debris.

Artist's illustration of a TransAstra mining probe. TransAstra is an asteroid mining company founded by Joel Sercel. EXPAT colonists will use the regolith left over from such mining operations to shield the habitat from harmful radiation.

We realized that this was a natural partnership. The byproducts of mining for water would provide us with shielding. You can see right there that you have the beginnings of an economic *engine* (driving force) in space. —Anthony

Expanding EXPAT's
shielding

Like everything on EXPAT, the shielding system is designed to be expandable. Each layer of the shield would be held in special bags.

The initial layer of bags might be filled with water, providing a basic level of protection from **radiation.** Inside this layer, workers would then lay in bags filled with **regolith.**

When the regolith layer is complete, workers would lay in another layer of empty bags, pumping the water from the outermost layer into this layer. This process would move the water layer inside the regolith layer. That way, if an object happened to strike and damage the outer layer, the station would lose a little cheap regolith, rather than leaking precious water.

The process could be repeated several times, each time laying in another layer of regolith, then pumping the water layer inside. At full thickness, the shield would provide just as much radiation protection as we enjoy on Earth.

> **"** If you're going to live there for a lifetime, you need about 16 feet (5 meters) of shielding. That is massive beyond imagination. **"** —Anthony

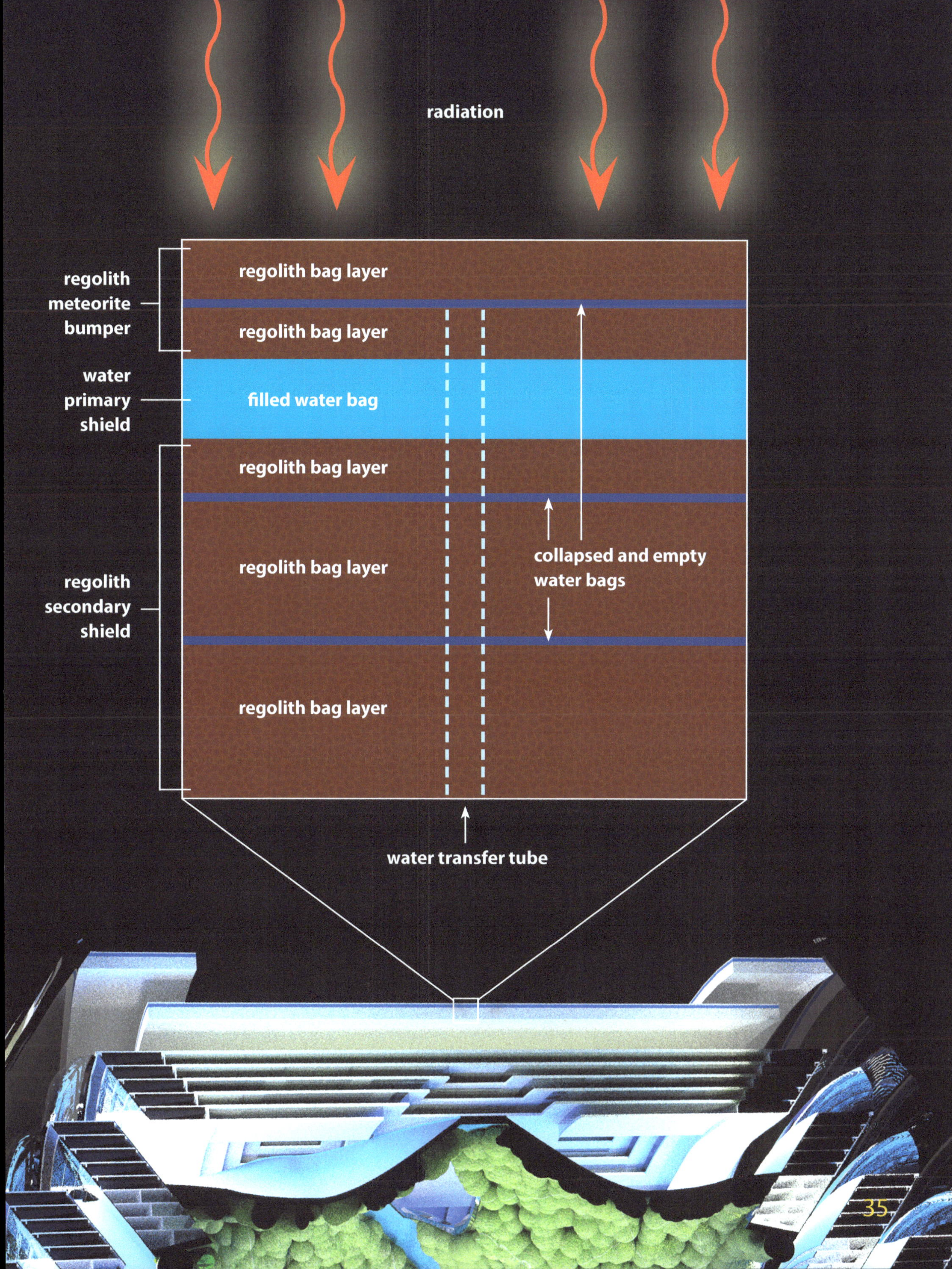

radiation
regolith meteorite bumper
regolith bag layer
regolith bag layer
water primary shield
filled water bag
regolith secondary shield
regolith bag layer
regolith bag layer
collapsed and empty water bags
regolith bag layer
water transfer tube
35

Bringing the great outdoors to outer space

One of Longman's goals for EXPAT is to recreate a beautiful outdoor area in space.

On the International Space Station (ISS), excess **carbon dioxide** and other gases are removed from the air using filters and scrubbers. Even the astronauts' urine is filtered to reuse the water! The filtration systems are amazing, but they have their limits. They require maintenance and repair and use up electric power and disposable cartridges. The ISS astronauts grow a few leafy greens as an edible experiment, but almost all their food must be shipped from Earth.

> ❚❚ You need the stability and *redundancy* (excess of resources) that an ecosystem provides. ❚❚ —Anthony

If a habitat as large as EXPAT worked the same way, it would need many tons of supplies delivered each year. Instead, EXPAT will be home to a balanced **ecosystem** of plants and other living things that will help clean the air, recycle wastes, and produce food without the need for constant resupply.

Creating such a balance will be difficult. Through experimentation, the ecosystem's designers will have to figure out the right mix of living things to send along with human colonists. Animals and plants in the "outdoor" section will have to be fast-growing and hardy, but not so aggressive as to wipe one another out. Plant crops will have to be selected to produce as much food as possible with limited resources.

A major difficulty of having such a vast open area is getting the gases to fill it. It would be extremely expensive to import all these gases from Earth. Also, the kinds of gases needed to produce an Earthlike **atmosphere** cannot be readily mined from **asteroids** or the moon.

Longman has developed a strategy to conserve the growing habitat's air supply. After the first few expansions, EXPAT's living space will be fitted with a clear membrane perhaps a half-dozen yards or meters above the habitat floor. This plastic "roof" will hold air close to the surface, leaving the open center of the growing habitat airless.

Longman's strategy will greatly reduce the amount of air needed while the habitat grows to full size. Eventually, EXPAT will acquire enough gas to fill the interior space. Then, the membrane would be removed and recycled.

The "outdoor" area will provide more than just life support. It will be essential for the mental well-being of EXPAT's human inhabitants. Being able to hike up a hill, play games outdoors, or just bask in the tall grass will help EXPAT's residents feel more of a connection to faraway Earth.

Night
and day

EXPAT will be designed to maximize the use of one of its most important resources: sunlight. The station will spin in such a way that its axis of rotation roughly lines up with the direction of its **orbit.** This will keep the shielded parts of the craft facing the sun, the primary source of dangerous **radiation.** But, two huge free-floating mirrors will orbit on either side of the habitat, angled to direct light through EXPAT's transparent sidewalls.

Continuous, diffuse sunlight would likely be unhealthy for the plants and animals—and people—living inside the habitat. Longman has an idea on how to create a nighttime and intensify the daylight. For about 12 hours, light would shine through specialized shutters to light the "outdoor" space. After that, the shutters would close.

Instead of blocking the light completely at "night," this system would redirect it to special farming areas lining the walls of the habitat. In this way, both the "outdoor" habitat and the farming sections would have a night and a day—just at opposite times.

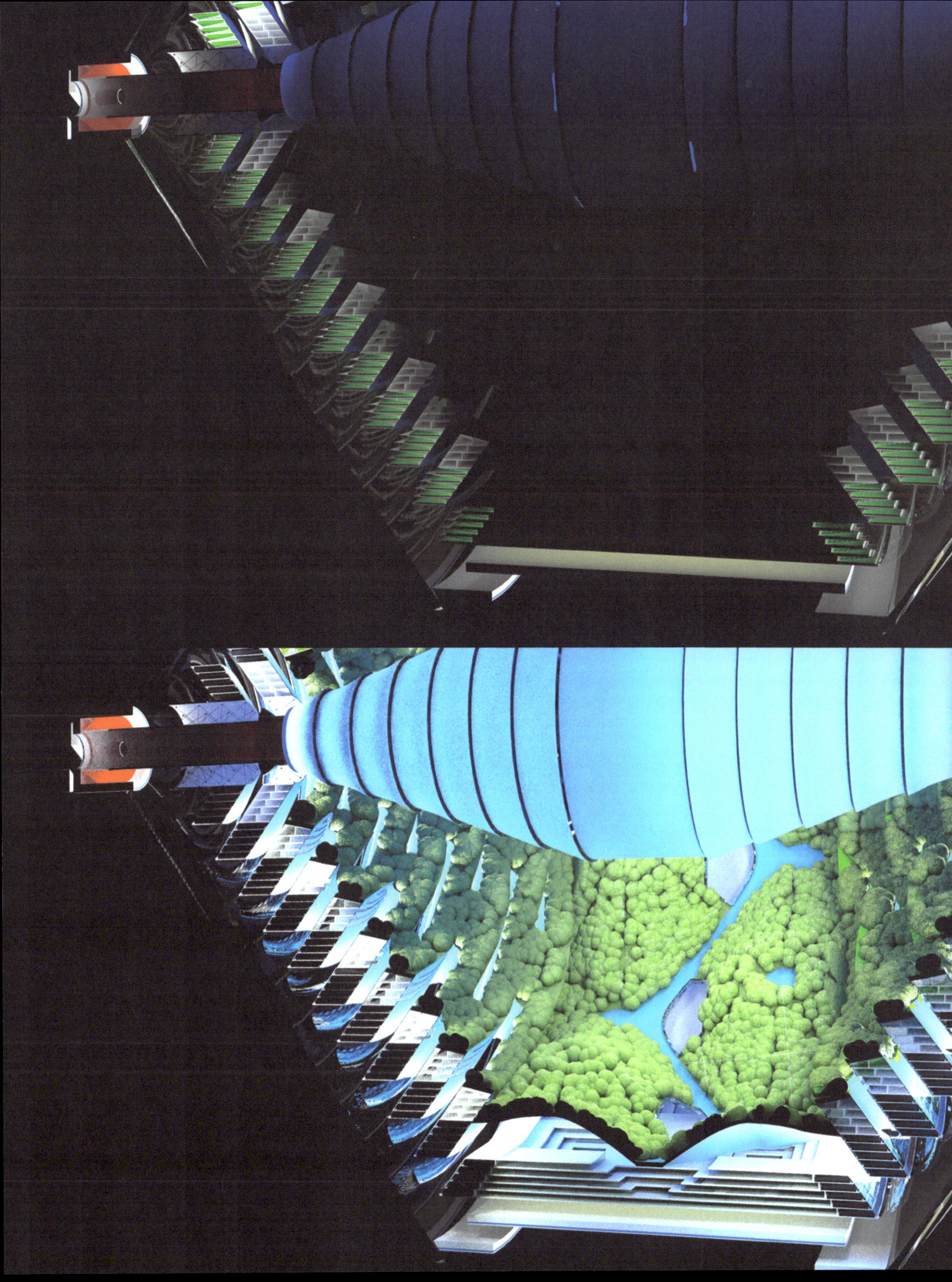

Final
form

In its fully expanded form, EXPAT will have three sections nested one inside another, somewhat like a traditional Russian nesting doll.

The outer section will consist of the **radiation** shield along with clear sidewalls to let in sunlight. This section is so massive that it will not spin.

Inside this will be the living area. This section will spin to produce artificial **gravity** and will be pressurized, allowing people to breathe. The "outdoor" section will house a beautiful **ecosystem,** complete with hills, ponds, and streams. Beneath that will be five or more floors of space where people will live and work. Along the sloping walls of the living area are stacks of "indoor" farms with smaller "outdoor" gardens on top.

The innermost section will be a weightless workshop, where scientists can conduct experiments and manufacturers can produce special materials. This section will not spin, but it will be pressurized. Each section will be connected to the next by two rotating *bearings* (guides) at the axis.

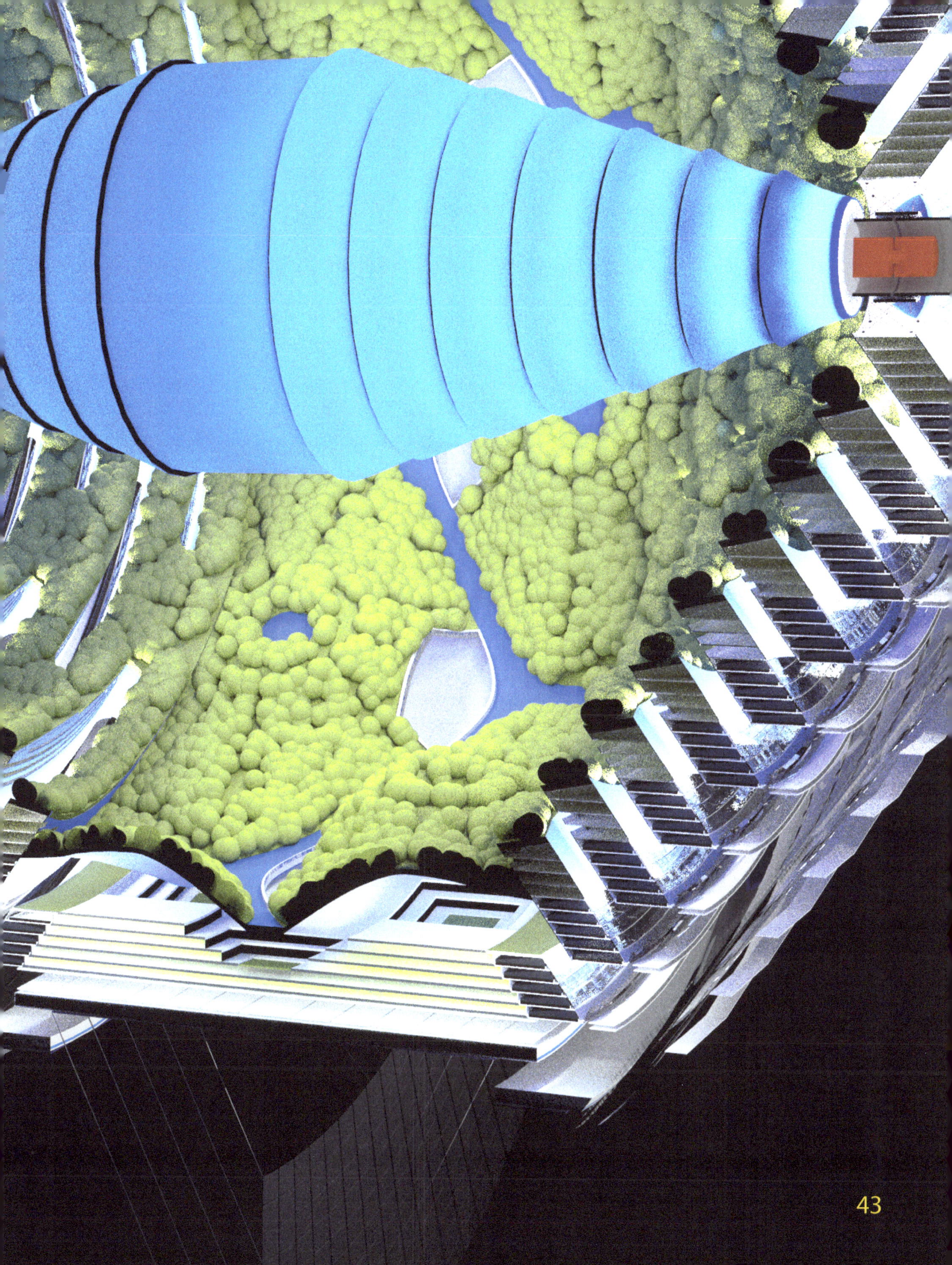

Inventor Feature: The structure of Bach

Longman's father was an avid collector of classical music and passed his love of the genre on to his son. Longman draws inspiration from the structure of classical music, especially the fugues of the German composer Johann Sebastian Bach (1685-1750).

Bach is considered the greatest genius of Baroque music, a highly complex and dramatic style of classical music that reached its peak in the early 1700's. In his compositions, Bach brought such musical techniques as counterpoint and fugue to their greatest heights. Counterpoint is the playing of two or more melodies at one time. Fugue is a composition in which one or more instruments repeat the same melody with slight variations.

Glossary

asteroid a rocky or metallic body smaller than a planet that orbits the sun.

atmosphere the mass of gases that surrounds a planet.

carbon dioxide a colorless, odorless gas present in the atmospheres of many planets, including Earth.

cycler a special orbit that passes two solar system bodies at regular intervals; a spacecraft in such an orbit.

ecosystem a system made up of living things and their *environment,* or the place they live. The living things in an ecosystem depend on one another and on their environment to provide the things that they need, such as food and shelter.

engineer a person who uses scientific principles to design structures, such as bridges and skyscrapers, machines, and all sorts of products.

gravitation also called gravitational pull or force of gravity, the force of attraction that acts between all objects because of their mass, or the amount of matter they contain. Because of gravitation, an object that is near Earth falls toward the surface of the planet. We experience this force on our bodies as our weight.

habitat living area.

landscape architecture a profession that involves the design and development of land for human use and enjoyment.

magnetic field the invisible area of magnetic influence, or effect, surrounding a magnet or magnetic objects.

orbit a looping path around an object in space; the condition of circling a massive object in space under the influence of the object's gravity.

propellant solid or liquid fuel that is turned into gas and put under pressure to push it forward.

prototype a functional experimental model of an invention.

radiation energy given off in the form of waves or tiny particles of matter.

regolith loose rock fragments, from large boulders to dust, covering solid rock.

tensegrity a principle of architecture in which structures are supported by rigid struts, under compression, connected by flexible cables, under tension.

Anthony Longman's EXPAT will be filled with colonists and private companies. In fact, its expansion hinges on attracting business to take advantage of the unique environment. Your challenge is to design a business for EXPAT.

STEP 1

Think about the challenge

Think about the kind of business you'd like to develop. Research the new kinds of products that could be made in space. But don't just confine your exploration to high-tech materials: could bagels baked in a weightless environment become the next big food craze?

STEP 2

Create your prototype

Plan your business by creating a flowchart of inputs, products, wastes, and costs. Who will your customers be? How will you get your products to them? Will your company need space in EXPAT's weightless workshop, the artificial gravity floors, or the farming areas? What resources will you need, and how will you get them? What wastes will you produce, and how will you get rid of them?

STEP 3

Share your design

Share your design with friends, classmates, or teachers. Imagine they're investors to whom you are pitching your idea. Create a presentation, perhaps with a slideshow or samples of the product. If possible, share your design with engineers, scientists, and entrepreneurs and ask for their input.

STEP 4

Grow your idea

Remember how Longman collaborated with entrepreneur Joel Sercel to improve the feasibility of both of their projects. See if anyone you shared your idea with will develop a business that works well with yours. See if one of your businesses can utilize the waste products of the other, just as regolith left over from Sercel's asteroid mining will shield Longman's EXPAT.

Index